CU00920482

Novels for Students, Volume 4 Copyright Notice

Copyright © 1999

Gale Research
27500 Drake Rd.
Farmington Hills, MI 48331-3535

ISBN 0-7876-2115-3
ISSN 1094-3552

Printed in the United States of America.
10 9 8 7 6 5 4 3

Like Water for Chocolate

Laura Esquivel

1989

Introduction

First published in 1989, Laura Esquivel's first novel, *Como agua para chocolate: novela de entregas mensuales con recetas, amores, y remedios caseros*, became a best seller in the author's native Mexico. It has been translated into numerous languages, and the English version, *Like Water for Chocolate: A Novel in Monthly Installments, with Recipes, Romances and Home Remedies*, enjoyed similar success in the United States. The film version, scripted by the author and directed by her husband, Alfonso Arau, has become one of the most popular foreign films of the past few decades. In a *New York Times* interview, Laura Esquivel told Marialisa Calta that her ideas for the novel came out of her own experiences in the kitchen: "When I cook certain dishes, I smell my grandmother's kitchen, my grandmother's smells. I thought: what a wonderful way to tell a story." The story Esquivel tells is that of Tita De la Garza, a young Mexican woman whose family's kitchen becomes her world after her mother forbids her to marry the man she loves. Esquivel chronicles Tita's life from her teenage to middle-age years, as she submits to and eventually rebels against her mother's domination. Readers have praised the novel's imaginative mix of recipes, home remedies, and love story set in Mexico in the early part of the century. Employing the technique of magic realism, Esquivel has created a bittersweet tale of love and loss and a compelling exploration of a woman's search for identity and fulfillment.

Author Biography

Esquivel was born in 1951 in Mexico, the third of four children of Julio Caesar Esquivel, a telegraph operator, and his wife, Josephina. In an interview with Molly O'Neill in the *New York Times*, Esquivel explained, "I grew up in a modern home, but my grandmother lived across the street in an old house that was built when churches were illegal in Mexico. She had a chapel in the home, right between the kitchen and dining room. The smell of nuts and chilies and garlic got all mixed up with the smells from the chapel, my grandmother's car-nations, the liniments and healing herbs." These experiences in her family's kitchen provided the inspiration for Esquivel's first novel.

Esquivel grew up in Mexico City and attended the Escuela Normal de Maestros, the national teachers' college. After teaching school for eight years, Esquivel began writing and directing for children's theater. In the early 1980s she wrote the screenplay for the Mexican film *Chido One*, directed by her husband, Alfonso Arau, and released in 1985. Arau also directed her screenplay for *Like Water for Chocolate*, released in Mexico in 1989 and in the United States in 1993. First published in 1989, the novel version of *Like Water for Chocolate* became a best seller in Mexico and the United States and has been translated into numerous languages. The film version has become one of the most popular foreign films of the past few decades.

In her second, less successful novel, *Ley del amor*, published in English in 1996 as *The Law of Love*, Esquivel again creates a magical world where love becomes the dominant force of life. The novel includes illustrations and music on compact disc to accompany it. Esquivel continues to write, working on screenplays and fiction from her home in Mexico City.

Chapters 1-4: Under Mama Elena's Rule

In Laura Esquivel's *Like Water for Chocolate*, the narrator chronicles the life of her great-aunt, Tita De la Garza, who lives in northern Mexico during the early 1900s. The novel's twelve chapters, written one per month in diary/installment form, relate details from over two decades of Tita's life, beginning in 1910, when she is fifteen years old, and ending with her death at thirty-nine. Each chapter also includes a recipe that Tita prepares for her family during this period. After her mother refuses to allow her to marry the man she loves, Tita channels her frustrated desires into the creation of delicious meals that often have strange effects on her family. Through the expression of her culinary art, Tita learns to cope with and ultimately break free from her mother's domination.

Tita is born on her family's kitchen table, amid the fragrant and pungent odors of cooking. Since Tita's mother, Mama Elena, is unable to nurse her, Nacha, the family's cook, takes over the task of feeding her. "From that day on, Tita's domain was the kitchen" and "the joy of living [for her] was wrapped up in the delights of food."

When Tita is a teenager, Pedro Muzquiz comes

to the family's ranch and asks for her hand in marriage, but Mama Elena refuses his request. Ignoring Tita's protestations, Mama Elena forbids her to marry, insisting that she abide by the family tradition that forces the youngest daughter to stay home and care for her widowed mother until her mother dies. Mama Elena suggests that Pedro marry Tita's sister Rosaura instead and Pedro agrees, deciding that a marriage to her sister is the only way he can stay close to Tita.

Mama Elena orders Tita to cook the wedding feast. As she prepares the cake, her sorrow over the impending marriage causes her tears to fall into the batter and icing. Nacha later tastes the icing and immediately is "overcome with an intense longing" as she thinks about her fiancé, driven away by Mama Elena's mother. The next morning Tita finds the elderly Nacha lying dead, "a picture of her fiancé clutched in her hands."

Tita now becomes the official cook for the ranch. Soon after the wedding, Pedro gives Tita a bouquet of roses to ease her depression over Nacha's death. She clasps them to her so tightly that the thorns cut her and she bleeds on them. When her mother forbids her to keep them, Tita mixes the petals in a dish that acts as an aphrodisiac for all who eat it, except Rosaura. Her eldest sister, Gertrudis, becomes so aroused by the meal that she runs to the outside shower, but the heat emanating from her body causes the wooden shower walls to burst into flames. Her body also exudes the scent of roses, which attracts a passing revolutionary. He sweeps her up still naked, on his horse, and rides away with her. When Mama Elena discovers that Gertrudis started to work at a brothel soon after her disappearance from the ranch, she disowns her.

The following year, Tita prepares the celebration feast for the baptism of her nephew Roberto, son of Pedro and Rosaura. Tita had been the only one present at Roberto's birth, which left Rosaura precariously ill. Since Rosaura had no milk after the birth, Tita tried to feed Roberto tea, but he refused it. One day, frustrated by his crying, Tita offers him her breast and is surprised to discover that she can nurse him. When Pedro observes Tita nursing his son, their secret moment together further bonds them. Tita's celebration feast generates a sense of euphoria in everyone who shares it— except Mama Elena, who suspects a secret relationship between Tita and Pedro. Her suspicions lead her to send Rosaura, Pedro, and Roberto to her cousin's home in San Antonio, Texas.

Chapters 5-8: Tita's Rebellion

After they leave, Tita loses "all interest in life," missing the nephew that was almost like her own child. One day rebels ride up to the ranch and ask for food. Mama Elena tells them they can have what they find outdoors, but they are not permitted in the house. Finding little, a sergeant decides to search inside. Mama Elena threatens him with her shotgun, and the captain, respecting her show of strength, stops the sergeant. Tita becomes even more depressed when she realizes that the men took the doves that she had enjoyed caring for. Later that day, as Tita prepares the family's meal, a servant appears and announces that Roberto has died because "whatever he ate, it didn't agree with him and he died." When Tita collapses in tears, her mother tells her to go back to work. Tita rebels, saying she is sick of obeying her mother's orders. Mama Elena smacks her across the face with a wooden spoon and breaks her nose. Tita then blames Mama Elena for Roberto's death and escapes to the pigeon house. The next morning, Tita refuses to leave the pigeon house and acts strangely. Mama Elena brings Dr. John Brown to remove her to an insane asylum, but, feeling sorry for her, he takes her to his home instead.

Tita is badly shaken and refuses to speak. As she sits in her room at John's home, she sees an old Native American woman making tea on the patio. They establish a silent communication with each other. Later she discovers that the old woman is the spirit of John's dead grandmother, a Kikapu Indian who had healing powers. John tells Tita stories about how his family had ostracized his grandmother and about her theory that all people need love to nourish their souls. When John asks her why she does not speak, she writes, "because I don't want to," which becomes her first step toward freedom.

One day Chencha, the De la Garza family's servant, brings some soup for Tita, and the food and Chencha's visit return Tita to her senses. Chencha then tells Tita that Mama Elena has disowned her. She also gives Tita a letter from Gertrudis, who writes that she is leaving the brothel because "I know that I have to find the right place for myself somewhere." Later, Tita accepts John's marriage proposal. When Chencha returns to the ranch, bandits break in, rape her, and attack Mama Elena, who is left paralyzed. Tita returns to care for her mother, who feels humiliated because of her nee d for Tita's help. Tita carefully prepares meals for her, but they taste bitter to Mama Elena, who refuses to eat them. She accuses Tita of trying to poison her so that she will be free to marry John.

Within a month Mama Elena dies, probably due to the medicine she was secretly taking to try to counter the effect of the poison she thought she was being given. Sorting through her mother's things, Tita finds letters hidden in her closet that tell of a secret love affair with a man of black ancestry, and of the birth of their child, Gertrudis. At her funeral Tita weeps for her mother's lost love. Pedro and Rosaura return for the funeral and Pedro is angry that Tita and John are engaged. While at the ranch, Rosaura gives birth to Esperanza who like Roberto, must be cared for by Tita, since Rosaura has no milk. Rosaura determines that her daughter, like Tita, will care for her and never marry, which angers Tita. When John leaves to bring his aunt to meet Tita, she and Pedro consummate their love.

Chapters 9-12: Tita's Fulfillment

Later, when Tita suspects that she is pregnant, Mama Elena's spirit appears, warning her to stay away from Pedro. Gertrudis, now married and a general in the revolutionary army, returns for a visit. After Tita relates her fears for her future, Gertrudis insists she must follow her heart and thus find a way to be with Pedro. One night Pedro gets drunk and sings love songs outside Tita's window. A furious Mama Elena soon appears to Tita and threatens her. When Tita tells her mother she hates her, her mother's spirit shrinks to a tiny light. The apparent reduction of Mama Elena's control relieves Tita, which brings on menstruation and her realization that she is not pregnant. However, the tiny light begins to spin feverishly, causing an oil lamp to explode and engulf Pedro in flames. As Tita tends to his burns, Rosaura and John note the strong bond that still exists between them. Upset, Rosaura locks herself in her bedroom for a week.

John has returned with his aunt, wanting to introduce her to his fiancée. Tita prepares a meal for them, knowing she will have to disappoint them by calling off the wedding. When Pedro argues with her because she is taking such care with John's feelings, Tita is angered that he doubts her love. "Pedro had turned into a monster of selfishness and suspicion," she muses. That same morning Rosaura finally emerges from her room, having lost sixty-five pounds, and warns Tita not to make Rosaura look like a fool by carrying on with her husband in public. That afternoon Tita receives John and his Aunt Mary, and confesses that she has lost her virginity and cannot marry him. She also tells him that she does not know which man she loves best, as it changes depending on which man is nearer. John tells Tita that he still wants to marry her, and that she would live a happy life if she agreed to be his wife.

The narrative then jumps to twenty years in the future as Tita is preparing a wedding feast. However, it is to celebrate the union of Esperanza and Alex, John's son. The death of Rosaura a year ago had freed Esperanza and Tita, making it possible for both to openly express their love. Tita's wedding meal again stirs the passions of all who enjoy it. Pedro's feelings for her, however, have been repressed too long; when he is finally able to acknowledge his passion freely, it overwhelms him and he dies. Devastated by his death, Tita eats candles so she can light the same kind of fire within her, and soon joins him in death. The sparks the lovers give off burn down the ranch. When Esperanza returns from her wedding trip, she finds Tita's cookbook and passes it down to her daughter, the narrator of the story, who insists that Tita "will go on living as long as there is someone who cooks her recipes."

Characters

Juan Alejandrez

Juan is a captain in the revolutionary army when he first sees Gertrudis. He is known for his bravery, but when he smells the scent of roses emanating from Gertrudis's body after she eats one of Tita's magical dishes, he leaves the battlefield for the ranch. Juan sweeps Gertrudis up on his horse and carries her away from her home and her mother's tyranny. The two later marry and return for a visit to the ranch as generals.

Alex Brown

He is the son of Dr. John Brown; his mother died during his birth. He marries Esperanza Muzquiz, daughter of Pedro Muzquiz and Rosaura De la Garza, at the novel's end.

Dr. John Brown

The family doctor who lives in Eagle Pass. When he comes to attend Rosaura after Roberto's birth, he is astounded by Tita's beauty as well as her ability to assist her nephew's difficult birth. He returns to the ranch when Mama Elena De la Garza calls him to take Tita to an insane asylum. He instead takes Tita to his home and nurses her back to health. Tita responds to his kindness and patience and agrees to marry him. His understanding of her dilemma after she confesses her infidelity with Pedro leads her to reconsider her decision to call off the wedding: "What a fine man he was. How he had grown in her eyes! And how the doubts had grown in her head!" At the last minute, however, she realizes that her love for Pedro is stronger than her affection for John.

Gertrudis De la Garza

Gertrudis De la Garza is Tita's strong-willed, free-spirited sister. The eldest of the sisters, she is a passionate woman who takes sensual pleasure in life. Tita's cooking arouses such strong emotions in her that she runs off with a soldier in the revolutionary army and thus away from her mother's oppression. When Mama Elena discovers that Gertrudis is working at a brothel soon after her disappearance from the ranch, she disowns her. Only after Mama Elena's death does Tita ironically discover that Gertrudis was the product of their mother's illicit affair with a half-black man. Gertrudis returns to the ranch after Mama Elena's death, now married and a general in the revolutionary army. She advises Tita to follow her heart as she has done.

Mama Elena De la Garza

Mama Elena De la Garza is the tyrannical, authoritarian, middle-class matron who runs her daughters' lives along with the family ranch. Not only does she enforce the tradition that compels the youngest daughter to care for her widowed mother for the remainder of her life, but she compounds Tita's suffering by forcing her to prepare the wedding feast for Pedro and her sister. Suspecting a secret relationship between Pedro and Tita, she sends Rosaura, Pedro, and Roberto to her cousin's in San Antonio. When Roberto subsequently dies, Tita blames her mother because she separated the child from Tita, who fed and nurtured him. Mama Elena doles out severe beatings and/or banishment from the family in response to any acts of rebellion. She beats Tita after the wedding guests eat Tita's meal and become ill, and breaks her nose with a wooden spoon when Tita blames her for Roberto's death. She banishes Tita from the ranch after Tita shows signs of madness and disowns Gertrudis for working in a brothel. Her need for control over her daughters is so strong that it does not end with her death. Her spirit appears to Tita to warn her to stay away from Pedro. When Tita refuses, Mama Elena becomes so angry that she causes Pedro to be severely burned. Her proud and stubborn nature also emerges after the bandits who raid the ranch injure her health. She feels humiliated by her need for Tita's assistance and thus cannot accept her daughter's offer of food and comfort—a rejection that ultimately leads to her death. Mama Elena does appear more human, though, when Tita discovers letters in her closet that reveal a secret passionate love affair from her past. After her lover and her husband died, Mama Elena suppressed her sorrow and never again was able to accept love.

Rosaura De la Garza

The middle of the three sisters, Rosaura De la Garza marries the man Tita loves. She causes Tita further pain when she determines that her only daughter will care for her and never marry, according to family tradition. Maria Elena de Valdes, in her article in *World Literature Today*, notes that Rosaura tries to model herself after Mama Elena in her treatment of Tita and Esperanza. She becomes, however, "an insignificant imitation of her mother. She lacks the strength, skill, and determination of Mama Elena." She also lacks her mother's passion. Tita discovers that Mama Elena has suffered from the loss of her true love and suppressed her emotions. Rosaura, on the other hand, never seems to display any capacity for love. Rosaura does, however, share some similarities with her mother. Like Mama Elena, she is unable to provide nurturance for her children. Tita must provide sustenance for both of Rosaura's children, just as Nacha had done for Tita. Also, Rosaura dies as her mother did, because of her inability to accept nurturance in the form of food from Tita.

Media Adaptations

- Based on Esquivel's own screenplay, *Like Water for Chocolate* was adapted as a film in Spanish by Alfonso Arau, starring Lumi Cavazos, Regina Tome, and Marco Leonardi, Arau Films, 1992; with English subtitles, New Republic, 1993.

Tita De la Garza

Tita De la Garza is the obedient but strong-willed youngest daughter of Mama Elena. On the surface she accepts her mother's dictates, even when they cause her to suffer the loss of the man she loves. Yet, she subtly rebels by rechannelling her feelings for him into the creation of delicious meals that express her passionate and giving nature. She obeys her mother's order to throw away the roses Pedro has given her, but not before she creates an exquisite sauce from the petals. Through her cooking, she successfully communicates her love to Pedro. Tita's caring and forgiving nature emerges as she takes over the feeding of Rosaura's two children when their mother is unable to nurse them and as she tends to her mother after being banished from the ranch. Even after Mama Elena accuses Tita of trying to poison her so she will be free to marry John, Tita patiently prepares her meals. When Rosaura suffers from severe digestive problems, Tita also comes to her aid. Even while Rosaura rails against Tita about her feelings for Pedro and threatens to send Esperanza away to school, Tita serves a special diet to help her sister lose weight and ease her suffering. Tita does, however, have a breaking point. Her strength crumbles when Mama Elena sends Pedro, Roberto, and Rosaura away, and later she hears the news of Roberto's death, which pushes her into madness. After she regains her sanity, she seems to redouble her will. She stands up to Mama Elena's spirit and thus refuses to be influenced by her. She also holds her own with Rosaura, and works out an arrangement where she can continue to have a relationship with Pedro and Esperanza. Her passion, however, is her most apparent characteristic. For over two decades, her intense feelings for Pedro never fade. Tita ultimately sacrifices her life for him when she lights herself on fire after his death so that their souls can forever be united.

Paquita Lobo

The De la Garzas' neighbor, who has unusually sharp senses. She is able to tell something is wrong with Tita when she is overcome by Pedro's presence at their first meeting. She also suggests that Tita appears pregnant at the very time when Tita suspects the same thing.

Chencha Martinez

A servant in the De la Garza household, Chencha becomes Tita's confidante. She takes pity on Tita after Mama Elena banishes her from the ranch and pays her a secret visit at John Brown's home. The soup she brings restores Tita's sanity. When she returns to the ranch, she is brutally raped, but is strong enough to survive the ordeal. Tita allows her to leave the ranch after this trauma, knowing that "if Chencha stayed on the ranch near her mother, she would never be saved." Chencha eventually marries her first love, Jesus Martinez, and returns to the ranch.

Morning Light

John Brown's grandmother, a Kikapu Indian, whom his grandfather had captured and brought back to live with him. Rejected by his grandfather's proud, intensely Yankee family, Morning Light spent most of her time studying the curative properties of plants. After her medicines saved John's great-grandfather's life, the family and the community accepted her as a miracle healer. While at John's home, Tita sees her, or her spirit, making tea on the patio. As Tita spends time with her, they establish a silent communication with each other. Her spirit helps calm Tita. Later John tells Tita about his grandmother's theory that we all need love to nourish our souls: "Each of us is born with a box of matches inside us but we can't strike them all by ourselves.… Each person has to discover what will set off those explosions in order to live." Tita comes to accept and live by this theory.

Esperanza Muzquiz

Pedro's and Rosaura's daughter. Tita insists that they name her Esperanza instead of Josefita, because she does not want to "influence her destiny." Nevertheless, Rosaura tries to impose on Esperanza the same kind of fate that Mama Elena imposed on Tita, but Rosaura's death frees Esperanza to marry Alex Brown, the man she loves.

Pedro Muzquiz

Pedro Muzquiz marries Tita's sister Rosaura only so he can stay close to Tita. He loves Tita, but shows little strength of character. He allows Mama Elena to run his life and separate him from the woman he loves. He also observes Tita's suffering under Mama Elena's domination and does little to intervene on her behalf. At one point Tita berates him for not having the courage to run off with her instead of marrying Rosaura. Marisa Januzzi, in her article in *The Review of Contemporary Fiction*, claims that "Pedro sometimes seems so unimaginative that only in fantasy … could such an underdeveloped male character and magical ending satisfy Tita."

Roberto Muzquiz

First child of Pedro and Rosaura. Tita establishes a mother-child bond with him when his mother is too ill to feed him. When Pedro observes Tita nursing his son, their relationship is further strengthened. After Roberto's death, Tita is unable to cope with the sorrow and descends into madness.

Nacha

Nacha cooks for the De La Garza family and their ranch. Soon after she is born, Tita establishes a close relationship with Nacha. Since Tita's mother is unable to nurse her, Nacha takes over the task of feeding her and exposes her to the magical world of the kitchen. During her childhood, Tita often escapes her mother's overbearing presence and finds comfort in Nacha's company. Nacha becomes Tita's surrogate mother and the kitchen her playground and schoolhouse as Nacha passes down traditional Mexican recipes to her. Unfortunately, Tita loses Nacha's support when, after tasting the icing Tita has prepared for Rosaura's wedding cake, Nacha is "overcome with an intense longing" for her lost love, and she dies of a broken heart. Her spirit continues to aid Tita after her death, however, coming to her aid when she is delivering Rosaura's first baby.

Narrator

Esperanza's daughter and Tita's grandniece. The narrator explains that her mother found Tita's cookbook in the ruins of the De la Garza ranch. Esperanza told her daughter the story of Tita's life as she prepared the cookbook's recipes. The narrator has combined those recipes and the stories her mother told her about Tita, explaining that Tita "will go on living as long as there is someone who cooks her recipes."

José Treviño

José Treviño was the love of Mama Elena's life. Because he was mulatto—half-black—her parents forbid her to see him and forced her to marry Juan De la Garza instead. Mama Elena continued a relationship with him, however, and Gertrudis is his daughter. Tita only discovers this secret relationship after her mother's death.

Themes

Duty and Responsibility

The first chapter begins the novel's exploration of duty, responsibility, and tradition as they present Tita's main conflict. Family tradition requires that she reject Pedro's marriage proposal so she can stay at home and take care of her widowed mother for the rest of her life. If she turns her back on this tradition, she will not fulfill what society considers her responsibility to her mother. Rosaura decides that she also will impose this tradition upon her daughter Esperanza and so prevent her from marrying Alex Brown. Tita recognizes, however, that the tradition is unfair; if she cannot marry and have children, who will support her in her old age? She tells Rosaura that she will go against tradition as long as she has to, "as long as this cursed tradition doesn't take me into account." Nevertheless, she and Pedro respect his duty toward his wife and child, for they remain discreet in their love as long as she lives.

Obedience

In order to fulfill her responsibilities toward her mother, Tita must obey her—a difficult task, given Mama Elena's authoritative nature. Mama Elena makes harsh demands on Tita throughout her life and expects her to obey without question. Mama

Elena feels that Tita has never had the "proper deference" towards her mother, and so she is particularly harsh on her youngest daughter. Even when Tita sews "perfect creation" for the wedding, Mama Elena makes her rip out the seam and do it over because she did not baste it first, as Mama instructed. After Mama Elena decides that Pedro will marry Rosaura, she insists that Tita cook the wedding feast, knowing how difficult that task will be for her. When Nacha dies, Mama Elena decides Tita must take full responsibility for the meals on the ranch, which leaves Tita little time for anything else. Tita's struggle to determine what is the proper degree of obedience due to her mother is a major conflict in the novel.

Cruelty and Violence

Mama Elena often resorts to cruelty and violence as she forces Tita to obey her. Many of the responsibilities she imposes on Tita, especially those relating to Pedro and Rosaura's wedding, are blatant acts of cruelty, given Tita's pain over losing Pedro. Mama Elena meets Tita's slightest protest with angry tirades and beatings. If she even suspects that Tita has not fulfilled her duties, as when she thought that Tita intentionally ruined the wedding cake, she beats her. When Tita dares to stand up to her mother and to blame her for Roberto's death, Mama Elena smacks her across the face with a wooden spoon and breaks her nose. This everyday cruelty does not seem so unusual, however, in a land where a widow must protect herself and her family from bandits and revolutionaries.

Victim and Victimization

When Mama Elena coerces Tita into obeying her cruel dictates, she victimizes her. Tita becomes a victim of Mama Elena's obsessive need for power and control. Mama Elena confines Tita to the kitchen, where her life consists of providing for the needs of others. She rejects Tita's individuality and tries to force her to suppress her sense of selfhood. Tita's growth as an individual depends on her ability to free herself from the role of victim.

Sex Roles

The novel closely relates Tita's victimization to the issue of sex roles. When Tita's mother confines her to the kitchen, she relegates her to a limited domestic sphere. There Tita's role becomes a traditionally female one—that of selfless nurturer, placing the needs of others before her own. In this limited role, Tita struggles to find a sense of identity. When Tita is taken to Dr. Brown's house, she marvels at her hands, for she discovers "she could move them however she pleased." At the ranch, "what she had to do with her hands was strictly determined." She learns of Dr. Brown's grandmother, Morning Light, who experimented with herbs and became a respected healer.

Topics for Further Study

- Research the rebellion against the Mexican government led by Francisco "Pancho" Villa and Emiliano Zapata. Explain how this rebellion provides an effective backdrop for the tensions in the De la Garza family.

- Explore Freud's psychological theory on the process of sublimation. Write an essay determining whether or not it can be applied to any situations in the novel. Use examples from the text.

- Investigate the term "magic realism." Read another work that employs this technique and compare it to *Like Water for Chocolate.*

- Research the position of women in

Mexican society in the early part of the twentieth century. How can your findings help define the novel's female characters?

Love and Passion

The forces of love and passion conflict with Tita's desire to fulfill her responsibilities toward her mother. In obeying her mother, Tita must suppress her feelings for Pedro. Her sister Gertrudis, on the other hand, allows herself to freely express her passion when she runs off with Juan and soon begins work at a brothel. Tita's and Gertrudis's passionate natures also emerge through their enjoyment of food. Both relish good meals, although Tita is the only one who knows how to prepare one. At one point, Gertrudis brings the revolutionary army to the De la Garza ranch so she can sample her sister's hot chocolate, cream fritters, and other recipes. The food analogy also applies to the love of John Brown for Tita. Although he is captivated by her beauty, he feels no passionate jealousy over her relationship with Pedro. He comes from a North American family where the food, as Tita finds, "is bland and didn't appeal."

Sanity and Insanity

As the need to obey her mother clashes with her own desires, Tita begins to lose her sanity.

When Mama Elena sends Rosaura, Pedro, and Roberto away, Tita loses all interest in life. The news of Roberto's death pushes her over the edge and she escapes to the pigeon house, refusing to come out. When John removes her from the oppressive atmosphere her mother has created, and he and Chencha offer her comfort and love, her sanity returns. Mama Elena never questions her own state of mind, although she is obsessive in her need to dominate her daughters. When Tita is found in the pigeon house, Mama Elena ironically states that "there's no place in this house for maniacs!"

Creativity and Imagination

Through Tita's creativity in the kitchen, she finds an outlet for her suppressed emotions. Thus, ironically, while Mama Elena tries to control Tita by confining her to the kitchen and forcing her to prepare all of the family's meals, Tita is also able to strengthen her relationship with others and to gain a clearer sense of herself. She pours all of her passion for Pedro into her meals, which helps to further bond the two. Her cooking also creates a bond with Pedro's two children, easing her pain over not being able to have children of her own with him. Tita's imaginative cooking is also a way for her to rebel against her mother; she recalls that whenever she failed to follow a recipe exactly, "she was always sure … that Mama Elena would find out and, instead of congratulating her on her creativity, give her a terrible tongue-lashing for disobeying the rules."

Supernatural

The final important element of the novel is Esquivel's use of the supernatural. Tita's magical dishes, which produce waves of longing and uncontrollable desire, become a metaphor for creativity and self-expression. Like an artist, Tita pours herself into her cooking and produces works of art that evoke strong emotions in others. Her careful preparation of her family's food also reveals her loving nature. Another supernatural aspect, the spirits of the dead that appear to Tita throughout the novel, suggest that one's influence does not disappear after death. Nacha's spirit gives Tita confidence when she needs it, much like Nacha had done while she was alive. Mama Elena's spirit tries to control Tita from the grave, making her feel guilty about her passion for Pedro.

Style

Point of View

In fiction, the point of view is the perspective from which the story is presented. The unique point of view in *Like Water for Chocolate* helps convey the significance of the narrative. Esperanza, Tita De la Garza's niece, finds her aunt's cookbook in the ruins of the De la Garza ranch. As she recreates the recipes in her own home, she passes down the family stories to her daughter. Her daughter becomes the novel's narrator as she incorporates her great-aunt's recipes, remedies, and experiences into one book. She justifies her unique narrative when she explains that Tita "will go on living as long as there is someone who cooks her recipes."

Setting

The turbulent age of rebellion in Mexico provides an appropriate setting for the novel's focus on tyranny and resistance. Soldiers, bandits, and rebels are regularly mentioned in the novel, and often make appearances important to the narrative. It is a bandit's attack, for instance, that compels Tita's return home after her mother has disowned her. As Pancho Villa's revolutionary forces clash with the oppressive Mexican regime, Tita wages her own battle against her mother's dictates.

Structure

The narrative structure, or form, of the novel intersperses Tita's story with the recipes and remedies that figure so prominently in her life. By placing an actual recipe at the beginning of each chapter, the author is reinforcing the importance of food to the narrative. This structure thus attests to the female bonding and creativity that can emerge within a focus on the domestic arts.

Symbolism

A symbol is an object or image that suggests or stands for another object or image. Food is the dominant symbol in the novel, especially as expressed in the tide. "Like water for (hot) chocolate" is a Mexican expression that literally means water at the boiling point and figuratively means intense emotions on the verge of exploding into expression. Throughout the novel, Tita's passion for Pedro is "like water for chocolate" but is constandy repressed by her dictatorial mother. An incident that symbolizes Mama Elena's oppression occurs when Tita is preparing two hundred roosters for the wedding feast. As she castrates live roosters to insure that they will be fat and tender enough for the guests, the violent and gruesome process makes her swoon and shake with anger. She admits "when they had chosen something to be neutered, they'd made a mistake, they should have chosen her. At least then there would be some justification for not allowing her to marry and giving Rosaura her place beside the man she loved." Food becomes a symbol of Tita's love for Pedro as she uses it to communicate her feelings. Even though Tita remains confined to the kitchen, her creative preparation of the family's meals continues to serve as a vehicle for her love for Pedro and his children, and thus as an expression of her rebellion against her mother's efforts to separate them.

Style

Magic realism is a fictional style, popularized by Colombian author Gabriel García Márquez, that appears most often in Latin American literature. Audhors who use this technique mingle the fantastic or bizarre with the realistic. Magic realism often involves time shifts, dreams, myths, fairy tales, surrealistic descriptions, the element of surprise and shock, and the inexplicable. Examples of magic realism in *Like Water for Chocolate* occur when Tita's recipes have strange effects on those who eat them, when spirits appear to her, and when she cries actual rivers of tears. The fantastic element in Tita's cooking is that it produces such strong emotions in her family. The art of cooking, however, does reflect the patience and talent of the cook—qualities that are appreciated by those who enjoy the results. The spirits who appear to Tita symbolize the long lasting effects of those who impact our lives and our own feelings of responsibility and guilt.

Foreshadowing

Foreshadowing is a literary device used to create an expectation of future events. In *Like Water for Chocolate*, foreshadowing occurs when John tells Tita about his grandmother's theory of love and life. She said that "each of us is born with a box of matches inside us but we can't strike them all by ourselves." We need the breath of the person we love to light them and thus nourish our souls. She warns, however, that lighting the matches all at once would be fatal. This process occurs at the end of the novel when Pedro's suppressed passion for Tita is finally "lit," and the intense flame is too much for him to bear.

Paradox

A paradox is a statement or situation that seems contradictory or absurd, but is actually true. The kitchen becomes a paradoxical symbol in the novel. On the one hand, it is a place where Tita is confined exclusively to domestic tasks, a place that threatens to deny her a sense of identity. Yet it is also a nurturing and creative domain, providing Tita with an outlet for her passions and providing others with sustenance and pleasure.

The Mexican Revolution

Although Mexico had been independent from Spain since the early nineteenth century, their governments were continually beset by internal and external conflicts. In the early part of the twentieth century, revolution tore the country apart. In November 1910, liberal leader Francisco Madero led a successful revolt against Mexican President Porfirio Díaz after having lost a rigged election. Díaz soon resigned and Madero replaced him as president in November 1911. Considered ineffectual by both conservatives and liberals, Madero was soon overthrown and executed by his general, Victoriano Huerta. Soon after the tyrannical Huerta became president, his oppressive regime came under attack. Venustiano Carranza, Francisco "Pancho" Villa, and Emiliano Zapata led revolts against the government. In 1914 Carranza became president as civil war erupted. By the end of 1915, the war ended, but Villa and Zapata continued to oppose the new government and maintained rebel groups for several years.

A Woman's Place

Richard Corliss, in his *Time* review of *Like Water for Chocolate*, writes that "Laura Esquivel brought Gabriel Garcia Marquez's brand of magic realism into the kitchen and the bedroom, the Latin woman's traditional castle and dungeon." Traditionally, a Latin woman's place is in the home. In the patriarchal society of the early part of the twentieth century, Mexican women were expected to serve their fathers and brothers and then when married, their husbands, sons, and daughters. These women often turned to the domestic arts—cooking, sewing, and interior decoration—for creative outlets, along with storytelling, gossip, and advice. As a result, they created their own female culture within the social prison of married life.

Maria Elena de Valdes, in her article on *Like Water for Chocolate* in *World Literature Today*, notes that little has changed for the Mexican woman. She defines the model Mexican rural, middle-class woman: "She must be strong and far more clever that the men who supposedly protect her. She must be pious, observing all the religious requirements of a virtuous daughter, wife, and mother. She must exercise great care to keep her sentimental relations as private as possible, and, most important of all, she must be in control of life in her house, which means essentially the kitchen and bedroom or food and sex."

Reading women's magazines became a popular pastime for many married Mexican women. These magazines often contained fiction published in monthly installments, poetry, recipes, home remedies, sewing and decoration tips, advice, and a calendar of religious observances. Valdes finds similarities between the structure of *Like Water for*

Chocolate and these magazines. She explains that "since home and church were the private and public sites of all educated young ladies, these publications represented the written counterpart to women's socialization, and as such, they are documents that conserve and transmit a Mexican female culture in which the social context and cultural space are particularly for women by women."

Critical Overview

When *Como agua para chocolate: novela de entregas mensuales con recetas, arores, y remedios caseros* by Laura Esquivel was published by Editorial Planeta Mexicana in Mexico in 1989, it quickly became a best seller. The 1991 English version, *Like Water for Chocolate: A Novel in Monthly Installments, with Recipes, Romances and Home Remedies*, translated by Carol and Thomas Christensen, also gained commercial success. The novel has been translated into several other languages.

Critical reception has been generally positive, especially when noting Esquivel's imaginative narrative structure. Karen Stabiner states in the *Los Angeles Times Book Review* that the novel is a "wondrous, romantic tale, fueled by mystery and superstition, as well as by the recipes that introduce each chapter." James Polk, in his review in the *Chicago Tribune*, describes the work as an "inventive and mischievous romp—part cookbook, part novel." Marisa Januzzi similarly notes in her assessment in the *Review of Contemporary Fiction* that "this short novel's got more heat and light and imaginative spice than the American literary diet usually provides."

Few scholarly articles, however, have been published on the novel. Molly O'Neill, in her interview with Esquivel in the *New York Times*, notes that American critics often consign the novel to the " 'charming but aren't we moderns above it' ghetto of magical realism." Scholars also may have avoided the novel because of what some consider its melodramatic tone. In a mixed review for the *Nation*, Ilan Stavans finds a "convoluted sentimentality" in the novel.

The articles that have been published praise the novel's cultural focus. Ilan Stavans, in the same *Nation* review, observes that the novel accurately "map[s] the trajectory of feminist history in Mexican society." Maria Elena de Valdes, in her article in *World Literature Today*, argues that the novel contains an intricate structure that serves as an effective parody of Mexican women's fiction. She also praises its main theme: "a woman's creation of space that is hers in a hostile world." Victor Zamudio-Taylor insists the work is one of those that "reactualize tradition, make different women's voices heard, and revitalize identity—both personal and collective—as a social and national cultural construction."

Esquivel's screenplay of *Like Water for Chocolate*, along with her husband Alfonso Arau's direction, helped the film become one of the most successful foreign films of the past few decades. Esquivel has also written the screenplay for the popular Mexican film *Chido One.* Her most recent novel, *The Law of Love*, again focuses on the importance of love and incorporates the technique of magic realism. Reviews of the novel have been mixed. Barbara Hoffert argues in her *Library*

Journal review that the novel "is at once wildly inventive and slightly silly, energetic and cliched." Lilian Pizzichini, however, writes in her review in the *Times Literary Supplement:* "Esquivel dresses her ancient story in a collision of literary styles that confirm her wit and ingenuity. She sets herself a mission to explore the redemptive powers of love and art and displays boundless enthusiasm for parody."

Sources

Marialisa Calta, 'The Art of the Novel as Cookbook," in the *New York Times Book Review*, February 17, 1993.

Richard Corliss, review of *Like Water for Chocolate*, in *Time*, Vol. 141, No. 14, April 5, 1993, p. 61.

María Elena de Valdés, "Verbal and Visual Representation of Women: 'Like Water for Chocolate,'" in *World Literature Today*, Vol. 69, No. 1, Winter 1995, pp. 78-82.

Barbara Hoffert, review of *The Law of Love*, in *Library Journal*, July, 1996, p. 156.

Marisa Januzzi, review of *Like Water for Chocolate*, in *Review of Contemporary Fiction*, Vol. 13, No. 2, Summer, 1993, pp. 245-46.

Molly O'Neill, "At Dinner with Laura Esquivel: Sensing the Spirit in All Things, Seen and Unseen," in the *New York Times*, March 31, 1993, pp. C1, C8.

Lilian Pizzichini, review of *The Law of Love*, in *Times Literary Supplement*, October 18, 1996, p. 23.

James Polk, review of *Like Water for Chocolate*, in *Tribune Books* (Chicago), October 8, 1992, p. 8.

Karen Stabiner, review of *Like Water for Chocolate*, in the *Los Angeles Times Book Review*, November 1, 1992, p. 6.

Ilan Stavans, review of *Like Water for Chocolate*, in *Nation*, Vol. 256, No. 23, June 14, 1993, p. 846.

Victor Zamudio-Taylor and Inma Gulu, "Criss-Crossing Texts: Reading Images in 'Like Water for Chocolate," in *The Mexican Cinema Project: Studies in History, Criticism, and Theory*, edited by Chon Noriega and Steven Ricci, The UCLA Film and TV Archive, 1994, pp. 45-52.

For Further Study

Mary Batts Estrada, review of *Like Water for Chocolate*, in the *Washington Post*, September 25, 1993, p. B2.

> This review praises the novel for its mixture of culinary knowledge, sensuality, and magic as "the secrets of love and life [are] revealed by the kitchen."

Stanley Kauffmann, review of *Like Water for Chocolate*, in *New Republic*, Vol. 208, No. 9, March 1, 1993, pp. 24-25.

> Kauffmann reviews the movie version of the novel and finds it "drawn-out' and "lacking in focus."